if you ever read a poem

GABY COMPRÉS

if you ever read a poem

for everyone who's believed in me and encouraged me in
the journey of finding my voice and myself in poetry.

for you, holding these pages. you give meaning to this gift
of sharing my words with the world. thank you for being
here.
i hope you stay a while.

for Gaby, age 18. and to think you didn't want to write a
book. look at you, look at us.
i am happy you listened to bravery.

to you:

if you ever read a poem, i hope it is beautiful.
i hope it makes you stop and think.
i hope it makes you say, 'thank you'.

if you ever read a poem, may it inspire you.
may it grow flowers inside your soul.
may it uncover feelings you didn't know you had.

if you ever read a poem, may it make you smile.
may it brighten your face.
may it bring out the joy in you like a summer sun.

if you ever read a poem, may it make you feel.
whatever it is you need to feel.
may it help you heal.

if you ever read a poem,
 may it grow something new inside you.
a song. a painting. a story. a poem.

i hope that such a poem finds you in these pages.

if you ever read a poem

if you ever read a poem

if you ever read a poem
i hope you read me.
i hope you find the poetry
that hides in my body,
my rhyming eyes, my dancing feet,
the curve in my lips,
the cinnamon of my skin.
if you ever read a poem
i hope you read me,
i hope you read the words
written on my skin,
how my eyes spell out the word 'light'
and how my hands speak of art
and my heart sings words like
bravery and hope
and if you ever read a poem
i hope it's me.

si alguna vez llegas a leer un poema

si alguna vez
llegas a leer un poema,
ojalá me leas a mí.
ojalá encuentres la poesía que se esconde en mi cuerpo,
en mis ojos que riman, en mis pies que solo saben bailar,
ojalá encuentres la poesía que se esconde
en la curva de mis labios y en la canela de mi piel.
si alguna vez llegas a leer un poema,
ojalá me leas a mí,
ojalá encuentres las palabras escritas en mi piel,
y veas como mis ojos deletrean la palabra 'luz'
y como mis manos hablan de arte
y como mi corazón canta de valentía y esperanza
y si alguna vez llegas a leer un poema,
ojalá sea yo.

my love is a four-year-old

my love is a four-year-old
on chocolate milk and cake
running way too much, way too fast,
giving way too much, way too fast.
it has the scrapes and bruises to show for it.
i have tried to put it to bed early,
to sing it lullabies
and read to it stories,
hoping for peace.

but my love goes to preschool,
where they teach it to write poems
and sing nursery rhymes.
in art class,
it spends the hour making paper hearts,
giving each one away and not keeping one to itself.
in music class,
my love learns to sing along with other hearts.

gaby comprés

on the report cards,
the teachers write that my love is impatient,
and it raises its hands too much,
wanting to give all the answers,
not afraid of being wrong.
the teachers tell me that math is not my love's strong suit,
that it mixes up its numbers
and always shares more than what it has.

 but they also tell me that my love
gives away all its snacks,
that it is an expert at holding hands,
at looking out for others and making friends.
the teachers tell me not to worry,
that a love like mine is gifted,
that when it is older it will change the world.
i tell them that i worry that my love is too much,
but they tell me that it is just enough.

heart and soul

i was born
with a heart too big to fit
inside my chest
and a soul bigger than my body
so i have chosen
to leave pieces of my heart
in the places my feet have known
in the people i have loved
in the words i have read
in the beauty my eyes have seen

and my soul

i have scattered it like seeds
and i have left parts of it
in songs,
in poetry,
in the laughter of children,
in the arms that have held me
and the hearts that have loved me

gaby comprés

poetry is

a bridge
between the heart and the mind
between my mouth and my fingers
between me and you
a song
a river
that leads to joy
a house,
my house
a city
with a million roads, all leading to my heart

roses and hello

after e.e. cummings's 'into the strenuous briefness'

how many hellos
has the earth heard?
how many beautiful beginnings
has she seen?
how many roses has she bloomed,
and how many of them have been gifted?
how many hellos
have given way to friendship and love,
how many of them have turned into light?
she keeps them all,
the roses and hellos,
turns them into poems
and turns them into time,
sunrises and sunsets,
beginnings and farewells,
you and me
between it all.

the story of a lifetime

you hold words
you hold worlds
you hold stories inside you
you are the beginning of a poem
the middle of a song
the end of a chapter
you hold unwritten letters
and filled journals
you are the story of a lifetime
your voice, the beginning of what could be
your eyes, the start of a fairytale
the stranger next to you on the bus, a main character
(maybe)
and all the 'what ifs' inside you, a thousand verses
your soul could color a thousand pages
your heartbeats could fill libraries
every beat, a word
every breath, a song
every step, a new page
every day, a beginning
every night, an ending
every moment, your story

i was alive

when the sun sets,
may those last rays of light
find me
and may they find me
with wild and bright eyes,
wind-caressed hair,
life-kissed cheeks.
may the sun know
that while it shone
i was alive.

gaby comprés

every now and then i let it go

i am not my body.
my soul is too big to fit inside it.
i have left my body many times
looking for a home for my soul.
i tried to make room inside other bodies
inside someone else's soul
only to get bruised and breathless.
i tried leaving my soul in places
but then when i left
i ended up missing it
so i brought my soul back to my body
it knows it is not its home
but it is the only home i know.
every now and then
i let it go
and it visits the stars.

what love looks like

when you go around looking for love
look for it first inside you.
it will be
(most certainly)
knocking at the door of your heart.
(your heartbeat)
let it in.
it will run through every room inside,
moving things around,
untangling the mess you've made,
making room.
it will change you.
you might not recognize yourself.
it will bring light to your eyes,
brighten your smile,
redden your cheeks.
it will teach you to make art.
to sing and write poetry and dabble in painting.
it will teach you to like you,
to love you,
the wonder that you are.
you'll know what love looks like
now that it's inside you.

gaby comprés

bravery looks good on you

bravery looks good on you.
it has brightened your eyes,
widened your smile,
opened your heart.
you walk with grace and grit
and your voice has learned to rise.
you have grown, not like a flower,
but the way trees do.
you have grown to be rooted and strong,
unafraid of the winds that try to scare you,
never bowing to their voices.
you have chosen to sing a song of courage,
to wear bravery like a crown on your head.
keep going.

i have seen your soul

i have seen your soul,
and it is the color of sunrise,
a gentle but burning fire.
i have seen your soul,
and it sings a song of bravery and joy.
i have seen your soul,
and it is a light, a star, the sun.
it shines, it heals, it loves.
i have seen your soul,
and it is a flower,
it grows, it blooms.
i have seen your soul.
it looks like hope.

gaby comprés

you are more than you know

one day
maybe
you will understand all that you are:
a never-ending story
a star in the night
and the night
and the sky
a flower
and the garden
and the earth
you are art
and the artist
the song
and the voice
you are more than you know.

if you ever read a poem

daughter // ii

they'll write poetry about you
about the way your hair danced with the wind
and the way your eyes turned into stars when the sun set
they'll make music out of your laughter,
of the sweetness and the life in it
they'll tell stories of your bravery and fire
and they'll be in wonder of you,
of the way you lived, the way you loved,
the way you were always tender when the world was
rough
they will remember you.

bloom

do not bury
what has been planted
in your soul.
it will still
bloom.

hair

i straightened my hair today
for the first time in three weeks.
my mother was happy
but i was not.

last night
she said,
i know you're an artist,
pero no andes como una loca.
don't go around looking like a crazy person.

i kept touching my hair today.
missing the stray curl that stayed behind my left ear.
missing the space my hair used to take up, wild and free.
feeling smaller.
in a body that was not my own.

gaby comprés

this hair, mami,
does not belong to an artist,
y no es de locas.
es mío; con él nací.
in it i carry the waves
that carry me
that carried the bones
of my ancestors all the way here.

these curls, mami,
they are strong enough to hold me,
to hold all that i am.
they are a garden in which beauty grows.
they are rivers that lead to the ocean.

if you ever read a poem

mi casa amarilla

viviré en una casa amarilla
pintada por el sol
una casa en la calle Alegría esquina Luz
y en mi casa amarilla habrá un jardín con flores
sembradas en amor y regadas con esperanza.
de mi casa amarilla hablará todo el mundo
y vendrán niños en bicicletas a ella
para conocer a la mujer con flores en su pelo
y estrellas en sus ojos,
la mujer que usa vestidos con bolsillos llenos de canela y
miel.

gaby comprés

my yellow house

i'll live in a yellow house
painted by the sun itself
a house that stands on the corner of
Joy Street and Sunshine Avenue
and in my house a garden will grow
with flowers watered with hope, rooted in love.
my yellow house will be the talk of the town
and children will come on their bikes
to meet the woman that keeps flowers in her hair
and a few stars in her eyes,
the woman that wears dresses with pockets
filled with honey and cinnamon.

if you ever read a poem

mis palabras son la lluvia

mi alma
se ha convertido en una casa con goteras
y mis palabras
son la lluvia que entra a través de ellas
y yo
yo intento atraparlas todas.

gaby comprés

my words are the raindrops

my soul
has turned into a house with leaks in its roof
my words
are the raindrops that fall through
and i
i am trying to catch them all.

if you ever read a poem

you will be the spring

let the poems
live in you.
let the words know you.
let them wear you
like a skin.
then
you will know them.
they will burst out from you
like flowers on the ground
and you will be the spring.

gaby comprés

milk and honey

do not let me give you
anything less than
milk and honey.
do not let me feed your soul
with emptiness.
empty words.
empty beauty.
empty love.
let every space that i fill
be occupied by a love
that was worth all we did to find it.
let me fill in the blanks you keep
with words that come from truth
let the beauty that i give you
mean something to you.

if you ever read a poem

for you
inspired by Rafaella

for you, for you, for you.
this is all for you.
the sun, the rain, the sky.
for you, for you, for you.
this is all for you.
the newness of every morning, the hope each sunrise
brings.
for you, for you, for you.
this is all for you.
the song in my heart, the song of the birds.
for you, for you, for you.
this is all for you.

this is your heart

there is room here for you.
this is your heart.
lean into it.
fill every space and don't fear
that you aren't enough to fill these spaces.
you are.
there is room here for you.
for your love, your fears, your bravery
and all that you are.
there is room here for you.
this is yours.
this is your heart.
grow here, in this earth.
let your roots find room to breathe.
this is your heart.
this is all for you.
rest your bones here,
you don't have to run.
this is yours.
this moment, this song.
it is all yours.

something

you tell me
you want to be something.
i see you and i tell you
that you already are
something
that you are much more than
something
that you are walking feet and a beating heart
and singing lips and a million stars
and a thousand songs
and you are the reason why some people wake up
in your smiling lips and your shining eyes
they find the sun
and your voice
is the song i want to hear forever
until i can sing along
and you want to be something
but you are so much more.

gaby comprés

instructions on opening the heart

whisper to it.
tell it you love it.
it will believe you, eventually.
sing to it.
until it is no longer afraid of your voice.
tell it about the world.
how it is graceful and beautiful and kind.
how the wildflowers grow.
tell it about this day.
how it is waiting for you.
how wonder calls your name.
tell it about love.
how it has been asking for it,
waiting for it,
homeless.

quédate

quédate,
a ver si la vida te sorprende.
a ver si el amor te encuentra.
quédate,
que el sol no tarda en salir,
y en la noche las estrellas brillarán para ti.
quédate,
que la vida es tuya,
que este momento es eterno.
quédate,
que hay cosas que no has vivido,
sentimientos que no has sentido.
quédate,
que nos falta camino,
nuestro destino aún no está escrito.

stay

stay,
let's see if life will surprise you,
let's see if love finds you.
stay,
for the sun will come out soon
and the night will shine for you.
stay,
for this life is yours,
and this moment lasts forever.
stay,
for there are lives to live,
feelings to feel.
stay,
there is a road ahead of us,
and our destiny is still unwritten.

the wonder

this is the wonder that's keeping the stars apart:
your heart, how it beats, how it sings.
your eyes, how they mirror your bright and wonderful
soul.
your feet, how they wander with no fear of what is to
come.
your soul, how it is the house of hope and freedom.
this, the you that you are,
is what is keeping the stars apart.
you are the wonder.

gaby comprés

you hold oceans

fun fact:
if you lay out your blood vessels
they are long enough to wrap themselves
around the world.
twice.
(i looked it up.)
love,
you are enough.
you hold oceans inside you.

soy mía

soy mía,
así como las estrellas son del cielo
y las olas son del mar.
soy mía,
como la luz es del sol
y al cielo pertenece el azul.
soy mía,
y soy de nadie más,
no vengo de ningún lugar,
solo de donde me quiera quedar.
soy mía,
intocable y vulnerable,
áspera y suave,
con el alma enredada en libertad.

gaby comprés

i am mine

i am mine,
the way the stars belong to the night
and the waves belong to the sea.
i am mine,
the way the light belongs to the sun
and blue belongs to the sky.
i am mine
and i am no one else's,
and i don't belong to a place,
only where i choose to stay.
i am mine,
untouchable and vulnerable,
rough and soft,
with my soul tangled in freedom.

when hands reach

after Sarah Kay's 'The Type'

when hands reach to touch you
may they reach for you
not hoping to find anything
but you
may they reach for you
knowing that you cannot fill empty spaces
and that you
do not have any empty spaces within you
may they reach for you
gently, in love,
with wonder.

to the psychiatrist who called me strange for not having a boyfriend

you know, i used to tell myself the same thing.
that maybe something was wrong with me.
that maybe love was enough for me but i was not.
i have imagined kisses a thousand times
i have dreamt of arms around my own
and i have written enough love stories for the entire world
and poems to fill books
and i have questioned so much-
my beauty, my worth, my skin, my bones
and i traveled and walked away
from fear and self-doubt
towards bravery and courage,
towards knowing what i wanted and what i deserve
and i know love is something i cannot earn,
something that belongs to me as much as air,
that love is enough for me
and i am enough for it
and i am enough with or without it.

ode to my heart

i have never written you a poem.
this is a song long overdue.
i love you
i love you
i love you.
i love you because you love
because without you
i could not love.
you are my needle and thread
the milk and honey that feeds these bones
the bread and wine of this soul.
you are the home of my words
you are the teacher of my hands
you tell them to hold other hearts gently
you tell them to hold on
you tell them to let go.
you sing to me every morning
you sing me alive
you sing to me
i love you
i love you
i love you.

gaby comprés

maybe love is in new york city

after 'when love arrives' by Sarah Kay and Phil Kaye

maybe love is in new york city.
maybe love is in paris.
maybe love is here.
maybe love has seen me
and secretly thinks i'm beautiful.
maybe love isn't as far from reach as i think it is.
maybe love plays the guitar or the piano
and has written songs about me
and the way my hair dances in the wind.
but maybe love is in new york city
waiting for me to visit.
waiting for me to take the train
waiting for me to make eye contact
while he sits on the opposite side of me.
maybe love is in new york city
or rome
or spain.
maybe love writes poetry
or short stories.
maybe love loves someone else right now.
maybe love will find me in five years
or in two months.
but love is out there.
maybe in new york city.

if you ever read a poem

beautiful day, hello

what will you give me today?
what song will you sing to me?
what surprises will you bring my way,
and how will you make my heart fall in love?

rain

i hope a rainy day
makes you smile,
that the sound of raindrops
makes you dream.
let the rain touch you.
isn't it beautiful to believe
that blooming isn't just for flowers
but also for you and me?

if you ever read a poem

every flower

every flower that blooms in me
comes from a seed planted in gratitude
the raindrops that fall on my earth
are whispers from my lips saying, 'thank you'

every smile born on my lips
was born first in the sky
my joy
is the light of a thousand stars

gaby comprés

i have been here before
after Sabrina Benaim's 'first date'

i have been here before.
this moment
is not foreign.
this moment
knows me
and i know it.
i have been here before.
i know this moon
and i know these stars.
they were shining over me
the night i was born.
their light is the same one
that lives inside me.
i have been here before.
the raindrops,
they know my skin,
for it is the earth that welcomed them in
when i became flowers.
i have been here before.

if you ever read a poem

here am i

here am i
a star lost in a constellation
unsure but shining
small but shining
lost but shining
shining
shining
shining
here
here am i
i am here
and i
i cannot be erased from this place
i cannot be removed
for i am a story
written with flowers and ink
with poetry and grace
with light and fire
and i belong here
here am i
i am here

gaby comprés

and i
i am a voice
a voice that cannot be quiet
a voice that sings the truths we like to forget
a voice that tells the stories of those who came
before me
before i was here
here
here am i
and i am not leaving

if you ever read a poem

you will find

when the last breath
leaves my lungs
bury my bones back in the earth
where i came from
plant me between seeds
and when you come back
you will not find me
but you will find beauty
you will find that life moves on
and keeps on growing
you will find
that endings are beginnings, too
and that stories are forever
when you come back
pick a flower,
put it in your hair
and i will be there.

daughter // iii

i thought of you today.
how you'll look like me
and probably have
my eyes
my nose
my skin
and my curls.
i'll tell you that they're beautiful
just like you
and your soul.
and you'll believe me,
because you'll live in a world
where the only thing that matters is
the beauty of your soul.

i hope

i hope you always find reasons to smile
that kind of smile that closes your eyes
i hope you always have a window to look out of
so that at night you can wish on stars
i hope you always find beauty in yourself
in your lips, in your eyes, in your heart
i hope love finds you
and that it never lets go
and i hope
i hope
i hope.

your heart is art

(your) heart holds every color of every rainbow
every wonder
every star
every song you ever sang
your (heart) holds every story you lived in
every place you were in
every word you ever spoke
your heart (is) this living, beating collage
of every moment
of everything you are
of everything you love:
the songs
the (art)
the magic of every second you are alive.

rain and stars
for Rai

you are rain and stars.
the goodness that falls from the sky.
you fall like raindrops
in my heart
like a song
the sound of heaven playing violins.
you are light
a shooting star
cutting through the darkness
turning it into magic
into beauty
into art.
you fall into my heart
like rain and stars.

gaby comprés

do not settle

do not settle for empty words
and empty beauty
do not settle for knowing what you know
and do not settle for the waves
when in the sea there is more below
do not settle for growing among roses
when you can grow tall among wildflowers
do not settle for a starless sky
do not settle for a love where there is no light
do not settle for words that do not move you,
for words that don't open the sky within you
do not settle
do not settle
do not settle.

if you ever read a poem

live for this

live for this,
for the beauty that hides in your days,
for the poetry, for the words that feed your soul.
live for this,
live for the music,
the words that echo what is in your heart.
live for this,
for the light, the hope, for everything beautiful given to
you.
live for this,
for the love, for it is what keeps you alive,
for it is what you are made of.

there isn't a part of you that is not worthy of love

i like you like this.
wild.
free.
unafraid and unapologetic.
i like you soft.
i like you brave.
i like your grit,
your whimsy,
the stars and fire that burn inside you.
i like you wholly.
there isn't a part of you
that is not worthy of love.

love is you

love is not a kiss
and love isn't only there when you are good.
love sees you and your brokenness
and love loves it
and love loves you
and love is you.

gaby comprés

hope is you

hope is not a feeling.
hope is you,
your heart and its beat,
your eyes and how they open
when the morning comes again.

if you ever read a poem

you are your home

don't run away from yourself.
you are your home.
come back.
closer.
take time to know you,
this marvelous and wonderful creation.
all you are is a mirror of goodness, of love,
of the hands that made you,
fearfully and wonderfully.

gaby comprés

enough

walk into this.
run, if you must.
and then, be still.
let truth fall upon you like rain.
let the drops turn you into oceans.
you are here.
you belong.
this is your soul.
walk down these halls
and touch the walls that carry your story.
know that you are enough
to take up all this room
and that you are worth it all.

i will not

i will never apologize
for the mess i am.
i will not tame
the wildness i carry,
the freedom i hold.
i will not change
the parts of myself you do not like.
i will not hide
the light i hold inside,
the sunrise in my soul.
i will not put out
the spark i kindled,
the fire i burn.
i will not silence
the song inside my bones.
i am this.
this is enough for me.

un jardín

no esperaré a que me traigas flores.
me convertiré en tierra
y sembraré en cada espacio de mi ser
rosas y amapolas y girasoles.
me convertiré en un jardín
y a lo mejor un día querrás pasear por aquí.
seré un jardín,
un faro en el mar,
una estrella fugaz en tu cielo apagado.

flowers

give me a love
that doesn't bring me flowers
. but instead
grows the ones i planted myself

these curls

these curls
these waves
they tell the story
of the people before me
how they came across the ocean
an ocean with waves like mine
these curls
they are springs
they are the spring
they are the life inside me
the earth that grows flowers
they are telling you that i am here
and that i am the story
the story of stories
the retelling of the lives that came before me
they tell of home,
of movement and flavor
these curls
they are mine
and they are good

woman

woman.
house of fire and hope
and light.
woman.
canvas where loveliness and fierceness blend.
woman.
ocean of flowers and life.
garden where all things wonderful grow.
woman.
you.

gaby comprés

you are an ocean

you are an ocean.
the waves.
the coming and going.
the falling and the rising.
the life underneath.

playing games with hope

we never tire of hoping,
you and i.
"if not today, then tomorrow.
and if not tomorrow, then the next day,"
we tell ourselves.
we like to play games with hope
and we always let her win.

gaby comprés

one day

one day
the rain will not be
water that makes the oceans
that drown you deeper
and the night will not be
the sheet that surrounds you in darkness.
one day
the rain will bring out
the spring inside you
and the night
will be the birthplace
of the stars within you.

love

Love will not have to
knock at your door if you choose
to leave it open

gaby comprés

my bones have been broken
so that light finds a way
through them

make this sorrow
this suffering
this pain
worth it.
tell me stars will be born
out of my darkness,
a spring from my winter,
wholeness from brokenness.
tell me
my bones have been broken
so that light finds a way through them.

grace looks like you

grace looks like you,
this beautiful thing that you are.
grace looks like you,
healing those who hurt you.

gaby compres

mosaic heart

heart broken
like shattered glass
all my pieces
thousands of stars
i held them
painted them
with grace and courage
put them back together
made myself a
mosaic heart
beating a new song
louder than before

if you ever read a poem

you've always been you

you've always been you,
you've always been this.
this wonder
this joy
this soul
painted in gold
painted in bravery
painted in joy.

gaby comprés

you cannot hide

what a beautiful thing it is
to be seen
to be known
to know
that you cannot hide
the color of your soul
the song in your heart.

if you ever read a poem

you've always been there

you've always been there.
you've always been what you are.
you are all of it,
what you were,
what you are,
what you will be.
you've hidden,
behind lies and fears.
you've put walls.
you've shown parts of yourself
but never the whole.
yet you are whole,
you are more than you know,
you are light and hope and love,
a song,
you are everything and more.

gaby comprés

the light has not hidden
its face from you

the sun came out and you were there to see it
do you know what this means?
the light has not hidden its face from you.

grow
for Manuel and César

you could
carry the whole world between
your tender fingers
this world
is not big enough for you
and the dreams you hold inside
but learn it,
get to know it
the way you know the back of your hand
let your eyes take in the beauty of all that is yours
so that your hands can paint it
and your fingers can write it
this world
is not big enough for you
but
it is your home,
it is where you grow
so, grow,
grow kind,
grow brave,
grow strong,
grow in love and in hope.

gaby comprés

write

write
the way you breathe:
always.
feel this, feel everything,
and then write.
feel the words
and how they wrap themselves around every moment.
how they shape your life.
how they hide between your breaths.
write
because when you are gone, your words will speak for
you.
write
because nobody else can write the way you do,
write
so that you don't forget yourself, your dreams, your hopes.
write
so that you don't forget this,
this moment
and the way your eyes glittered like stars.
write
so that your words fly to those places
your voice cannot reach.
write
the way you breathe:
always.

if you ever read a poem

this is all free

i am a world of stories.
my imagination
a sea of words.
come away with me.
we will travel
over mountains of make-believe,
discover ourselves
in forests of fairytales,
in clouds of song.
this is all free.

gaby comprés

the world needs me like this

overtrusting, me? yes.
naïve? i am a little bit of that, too.
but the world needs me like this.
hopeful. kind.
the earth needs me to believe in her,
in the kindness of her people,
the love inside them.
if i believe it myself, maybe they'll believe it, too.

if you ever read a poem

quiero darte una canción
para Denisse

quiero darte una canción.
que la cantes en la mañana.
que el gallo se despierte con tu voz,
que el sol salga para escucharte.
quiero darte una canción,
quiero darte alegría.
quiero darte palabras,
un poema, la libertad de cantar.
quiero darte una canción.
que la cantes en la tarde,
cuando cueles el café y te sientes a ver el mundo pasar,
cuando los niños que juegan en la calle te saluden,
y que ellos canten también.
quiero darte una canción,
que la cantes en la noche.
que el sol cante tu canción a la luna
y ella salga a verte a ti.

gaby comprés

i want to give you a song
for Denisse

i want to give you a song.
sing it in the morning,
let the rooster wake up with your voice,
let the sun come out to hear you sing.
i want to give you a song,
i want to give you joy.
i want to give you words,
a poem, the freedom to sing.
i want to give you a song.
sing it in the afternoon,
when you put on the coffee
and you sit down to watch the world,
when the children that play in the street wave at you,
let them sing too.
i want to give you a song.
sing it in the night.
let the sun sing your song to the moon.
let her come out to see you.

café

el café de las seis de la mañana,
para despertar al sueño.
el café de la una,
para despertar los ánimos.
el café de las cuatro,
para despertar los poemas.
el café, a cualquier hora:
para despertar el alma.

gaby comprés

coffee

six in the morning coffee,
for waking up dreams.
one in the afternoon coffee,
for waking up spirits.
four in the afternoon coffee,
for waking up poems.
coffee, at any time:
to wake up the soul.

how beautiful

how beautiful it is
to grow, to change.
to come closer to the person you've wanted to be.
who you've been all along.
how beautiful it is
to choose joy and have joy choose you back.
to find the sun inside you,
and flowers growing out of your heart.
how beautiful it is
to fall in love.
with places, with people.
with yourself.
to find beauty in the streets of your city.
to let wonder surprise you.
how beautiful it is to be.

gaby comprés

sparrows

the sparrows and their song
visited my windowsill this morning
their notes
a poem
a memory
a whisper,
"we are here, we sing.
you are here, so sing."

que tus ramas puedan
tocar el cielo
a Carmen

que te queden muchos atardeceres por ver.
muchos sentimientos
y pocas palabras para expresarlos.
que te sobren los deseos de ver el sol salir de nuevo,
que los cielos estrellados te hagan sonreír.
que te sobren razones para abrir los ojos,
para respirar.
que la vida te sonría,
que nunca dudes de si te aman.
que tus pies no le teman al camino desconocido,
y que a tus ojos no les queden lugares sin ver.
que la tierra donde te han sembrado
sea tan profunda como tus raíces,
pero que tus ramas puedan tocar el cielo.

gaby comprés

may your branches
touch the sky
to Carmen

may you have a thousand sunsets yet to see
many feelings and few words to explain them.
may you always want to see the sun rise again
and may a starry night bring out a smile.
may there be more than enough reasons to open your eyes.
may life smile at you
and may you never doubt that you are loved.
may your feet not be fearful of the unknown path ahead
and may your eyes see every wonder there is to see.
may the earth you are planted in be as deep as your roots
but may your branches touch the sky.

if you ever read a poem

so much depends

today i have the sun
on the tip of my tongue
and i am tasting the possibilities
and the wonder
that live in this day.
can you taste it too?
how this day can end so differently from how it begins,
how so much depends on you and me,
how so much is still unwritten?

my love

my love
will write you poetry
my love
will paint you yellow on rainy days
my love
will taste like coffee
my love
will grow flowers on your bones
my love
will know every strand of your hair
and every freckle on your skin
my love
will love you in english, in spanish
and the bits of mandarin and portuguese and french
i remember.
my love
will light up your soul like stars in the sky
my love
will learn all your favorite songs just to sing them back
my love
will love you
my love
won't change you
it won't try to make you fit
in places where you don't.

if you ever read a poem

when i'm with you

when i'm with you
and you look at me
i know you see me
the way i have always seen myself
when i'm with you
i feel like i am every star in the sky
and when i'm with you
i feel infinite and more than what i am
i forget my feet because you give me wings
and i am not afraid to fly
when i am with you
you turn into rain and i turn into flowers

keep my heart

i will stretch my heart,
make it reach wherever you are
for my love will never leave you:
it cannot be where you are not.
you will find it in yellow flowers
when you walk down the streets,
in golden sunsets and green leaves.
i hope you keep my heart (inside yours)
i hope you keep me like a song:
sing my words, sing my love.
keep my heart inside your heart
and i will be where you are.

everywhere everywhere everywhere

they buried your bones,
but not what was inside them.
they buried your bones,
but they didn't
they couldn't
bury your light, your love,
the story you told while breath was still yours
they didn't
they couldn't bury your laughter,
your song,
the memories the ones that loved you keep.
they buried your bones
but they didn't
they couldn't bury you,
for you are not there,
in those underground houses of dirt.
you are in the hearts of those who loved you,
in the faces of your children,
in your grandchildren's eyes.
you are in the words you said,
the places your feet touched.
you are
everywhere
everywhere
everywhere

gaby comprés

hearts grow together

what is it about distance
that makes hearts grow together
even though they are apart
your heart
thousands of miles away
from mine
and i hear it beat
as if you were right next to me

if you ever read a poem

come alive

you are poetry on a rainy afternoon
the smell of coffee in the morning
you are the sunlight that floods my room,
making everything inside me
come alive

forever

forever is this.
this moment in which your smile
reaches your eyes
and laughter escapes your mouth
like a river rushing to the sea.
forever is this.
the music that makes your soul sing,
the moments in which stillness finds you.
forever is this.
this feeling in which you have never been more certain
that you are here, that you are alive.

if you ever read a poem

everything and everywhere

i am finding you
in places i didn't think i would
like myself
and in hearts that beat like mine
i am finding you
and knowing that i will never finish knowing you
because you are
everything and everywhere

gaby comprés

alive alive alive

i saw God today.
he was in a coffee shop and a baseball game.
he was the light in your eyes,
the curve of your smile,
the salt in your tears.
i heard him
in my broken prayers
and the sound of your laughter.
between my breaths and your own.
i saw him
in the orange of sunsets.
i felt him
in your arms.
alive alive alive.

if you ever read a poem

there is only light

if you
looked inside my soul
i am sure
it would be
yellow.
in it
there is only light.

gaby comprés

in your time

lean into this,
the hard work
the heart work
the artwork
of growing.
know that this isn't forever.
your body, your home will catch up
to the blossoming of your soul.
days and months and years will pass.
but then, like a child, like a flower in spring,
you will bloom, you will rise.
here.
unrushed.
in your time.

vulnerability

vulnerability is a risk.
it might break you.
but through the cracks is where the light shines.
vulnerability is a game
and no matter how much you lose
you will always win.
vulnerability might wound you,
but it will heal you, too.
don't run away from this,
don't walk away from it.
come closer, dip your toes in this water.
know that this is how you grow,
how you love,
how you become into what you will be.

gaby comprés

freedom is not far

don't lose time
don't lose yourself
in places
where you know your heart does not belong
go to where your heart is free
come closer
to who you are
find yourself
in places where your smile shines,
go to where your eyes
light up like a night sky,
where your laughter sounds like a song.
freedom is not far.

the blooming

the blooming will surprise you.
you will open your eyes one day
and finally see
who you've been all along
and you will notice only
when your light has become too bright to hide.
the blooming will come
when you least expect it
when the petals of your flower heart
have surrounded your soul.
the blooming will make you forget
the pain that came before.
the blooming will find you
with laughter and joy bubbling from your being
flowing like a river,
the blooming will find you
with light swimming in your eyes,
with the sun inside your soul.

gaby comprés

sometimes

sometimes it looks like waking up.
sometimes it looks like opening the windows and letting
daylight in.
sometimes
sometimes it looks like smiling at strangers
like saying 'yes'
like saying 'no'.
sometimes it's big
like buying the plane ticket
quitting your job
falling in love.
sometimes it looks like singing a song
writing the words
or saying them out loud.
sometimes it looks like moving
sometimes it's staying.
sometimes
sometimes it's small.
like saying 'hello'
like walking inside
or stepping out.
sometimes it's an easy choice.
sometimes it's not.
but it is always worth it.
and it is all courage.

if you ever read a poem

glory and stars and grace

here we are.
and i don't know if we understand
the power of that,
if we understand
the wonder,
the odds,
the millions of seconds
and everything that had to happen
for us to be here.
we are walking miracles,
we are breathing art,
we are glory and stars
and grace
living inside a house of bones and flesh.

i'll be the sky

for you
i'll be the sky
i'll wear the stars on my skin
and let you wish upon my light

i love you

if i ever told you
i loved you
i meant to say
'thank you'
for not running away
for looking at me and choosing to stay
what i meant to say
was that
my heart has found a home inside yours
when i tell you i love you
what i mean is that
you are an ocean i am not afraid of drowning in
what i mean is that
i have never been afraid of being alone
but when i'm without you
loneliness tastes like bitter coffee
when i say i love you
i mean it.

the you that you are

the you that you are
is
the you that i want
wild and brave and soft
kind and alive and hopeful
the you that you are
makes
the me that i am
wild and brave and soft
kind and alive and hopeful
because of
the you that you are
i am the me that i am

if you ever read a poem

you do not have to be who you were

you are allowed
to grow,
to bloom,
to change,
isn't that what life is for?

time does not pass by in vain.
time tangles its fingers through your hair
threads them between yours
hoping not to leave you untouched,
unchanged.

do not ask
if there is room for you
everything here to you belongs
every color is for you to paint with
everything you can be you already are

and you do not have to be who you were.

gaby comprés

cause for celebration

i ask only one thing
from life:
that it surprises me.

it always does,
with the sun
and the thousand colors
that live in the sunrise

the birds
and how they sing
for me
to know that they are here

every morning
every breath
is cause for celebration.

if you ever read a poem

waiting for wonder

the sky was blue
the way it is before it goes to sleep
and an airplane crossed it
and she said,
"look! an airplane!"
and her voice carried a song
the way we did when she was four and i was five
and airplanes were birds that flew across our skies
magic cars that touched the stars
now we are twenty and twenty-one
waiting for wonder to fill us again
but now i know it lives
in blue skies that are almost asleep

gaby comprés

this is my heart

this is more than a song.
this is more than poetry.
this is my heart.
every day i break it
turn its pieces into words
that will make the pieces of your broken heart
put themselves back together.

if you ever read a poem

quiero

quiero tejer las estrellas entre tu pelo
bañar tu boca en miel
quiero pintar tu corazón
escribir poesía por toda tu piel
quiero esconderme detrás de tus párpados
sembrar flores en tus huesos
quiero vivir en tu pecho
y tus heridas taparlas con besos.

gaby comprés

i want

i want to braid the stars between your hair
and dress your lips with honey
i want to paint your heart
and write poetry across your skin.
i want to hide behind your eyelids
and grow flowers on your bones
i want to live on your chest
and heal your scars with my lips.

this is our beauty

this is our beauty,
that we are what we are.
that we are here,
breathing grace and shining among stars.
this is our beauty,
that we grow among flowers
and feel the sunlight on our skin.
this is our beauty,
that when the rains come
we don't run,
we stay rooted in this earth.
this is our beauty,
that we are here,
that our stories are being written
and woven together
like threads of the most beautiful tapestry.

gaby comprés

i am the poem

sometimes i try too hard
at making poetry out of nothing
not realizing
that sometimes, i am the poem
the words are in my bones
and the rhyme in my eyes and knees
the life in my feet
and the beauty is in every freckle
and bit of cinnamon skin
sometimes beauty is not outside
sometimes it hides within

if you ever read a poem

the stars come out to see you

every night
you go outside
to see the stars
but,
don't you know?
they come out to see you.

gaby comprés

you are most beautiful

you are most beautiful
when you smile
and nobody is watching
when you let yourself be surprised
by joy, by hope
when life finds you right in its middle
and you cross my sky
like a shooting star
you are most beautiful
when you sing your song
and you do not stop to see
if the world is singing along
you are most beautiful
when you are too occupied being yourself
to notice that you have turned into a butterfly
you are most beautiful now.

if you ever read a poem

what are you doing with your voice?

birds sing
to love
to say,
'i am here and this is my world'
and you, lovely thing,
what are you doing with your voice?

i am lucky to know a poet
for Michael

i am lucky to know
a poet
my poet has taught me
to look
at the world as if it were
a garden
a garden that is blooming words
like flowers
waiting for me to pick them and
arrange something
my poet has taught me
to stop
to look around me with eyes and heart
wide open
my poet has taught me
to breathe
to let in all the beauty in store for me
to listen
to the birds and their songs
to feel
to let the world be
to be
i am lucky to know
a poet.

if you ever read a poem

paper heart

'this is my heart,' i tell you.
you hold it between your hands.
'be gentle, be kind, be soft,' i want to tell you.
i smile,
i let you believe it is strong and unbreakable.
but this heart,
my heart,
is made of paper,
light, fragile and easily breakable.
it is bendable,
and often tries to fold itself and look smaller than what it
is.
an origami heart.
when you unfold it,
you can see the creases love left,
you can trace with your hand the exact place where pain
left its mark,
you can read the stories left in the lines.
and still,
despite it all,
my origami heart, my paper heart
is a work of art.

i am

i am
the songs my heart whispers
when no one else is around to listen
the words i have not learned to write yet
i am heavy and light
unfinished and complete
small to fit in the palm of your hand
and with enough light to be every constellation
i am
the faith that dances inside my soul
the flowers the rains make bloom
the hope i have not lost

more than this

i am more than this.
more than the night in which
my tears fall like rain,
watering the soil that is my soul.
i am more than this.
more than the words i do not know yet,
the feelings i cannot sing.
i am more than this.
more than the stars that
turn the night into day.
i am more than this.
more than this moment,
and all the ones before it.

gaby comprés

hope grows

hope grows.
it does not know how to stop,
it is not afraid of what is to come.
it runs towards tomorrow,
its darkness and light,
and into the unknown.
still, hope grows.
unafraid of the pain,
knowing there is grace underneath,
knowing that spring is near,
that everything beautiful lies on the other side of fear.
still, still and still,
hope grows.

here we are // i

here we are.
trying to fill the emptiness
the places where we hurt each other
with small talk
and offerings of cups of coffee
and chocolate cake slices
and flan
as if the sweetness
is enough to cover our faults.
as if sugar is the cure
for the wounds we keep.
and today.
it is.
it is a place to start.

gaby comprés

maybe you'll let them bloom

i'll always believe that my love was never wasted on you.
that even though i have chosen to leave you,
i left seeds under your ground.
maybe you'll let them bloom.

maybe one day

maybe one day
i will run out of words for you
and my heart will learn not to fill
the empty spaces
with poems you will never read
maybe one day
the longing will be filled
maybe it will turn into a memory
and my days will no longer
be tinted with its color
maybe one day
i will learn to let you go
maybe i won't have to
maybe one day
the sun will stop telling me
that another day went by without you here
and it will only mean
another day
maybe one day
i will only find metaphors in poetry
and not in your absence

gaby comprés

hands

my hands are like my heart:
they know how to hold heaviness.
they know how to hold hope.
they make words come alive.

my hands, like my heart,
have learned to let go.
to hold on.
they have learned not to be so soft but not too rough.

both of them, my heart and my hands,
they are like hummingbird wings.
they flutter, they dive into love as if it were an ocean.
they do not know how to stop.

the milk to my coffee

i don't want you to be
the sun to my sunflowers
i don't want you to be
something i can't rise without
and i don't want to
die
should you choose to leave me
maybe you can be
the milk to my coffee
with you i'll be sweeter, lighter
but
without you i'll still be strong

gaby comprés

love like

aren't you tired of looking for love?
aren't you tired of waiting for it?
the love like a movie like a song
like a story like a dream like a poem?
aren't you tired?
isn't your hope weary?
and, don't you see?
love has always been here,
the love you crave,
the love like a movie like a song
like a story like a dream like a poem
love like a river like a waterfall like an ocean
love like this morning like this breath like this moment?
love like this
like you
like me.

here we are // ii

here we are.
mending our broken hearts
putting together the shattered bits
with needle and threads
of stories and laughter
healing,
slowly.
but healing.

gaby comprés

i'll be here waiting

i'll be here waiting,
like a poem in a book,
waiting for the right time
for the words to mean something
to you.
i'll be here waiting,
like the light of a dying star,
still shining long after its life went out.
i'll be here waiting,
like a river
showing you the way to the sea.

if you ever read a poem

i am everywhere

i am everywhere.
in the sun.
in lavender skies.
in the words i write,
the words i haven't written yet,
the words i don't know.
i am everywhere.
caught up in my past.
looking forward.
here.
i am everywhere.
in the sky.
in this earth.
wandering and rooted.
i am everywhere.
lost.
finding myself.
found.
i am everywhere.

gaby comprés

all i am

i want the words
for all i am,
the ocean that dances
inside me,
the waves that i cannot stop from rushing.

if you ever read a poem

looking for myself

i am looking for myself,
finding bits of my soul
in the waves of the sea,
the light of the stars,
the glow of the sun.
i am looking for myself,
falling in love
with the shape of my bones,
the dancing of my curls with the wind
and the earth that is my skin.
i am looking for myself,
reading the words that make my story,
the poetry that is between my breaths,
between my heartbeats
and tangled in my soul.

gaby comprés

the water speaks to me

my mother loves the ocean
and the song it sings to her
of peace
and the water speaks to me too
in the language of rain,
of april and may,
flowers and spring.

áfrica

sobre mi pierna derecha,
debajo de mi rodilla,
vive una mancha color canela
que se parece un poquito a áfrica
así como yo me parezco a áfrica
en la forma de mi nariz
y en las olas de mis rizos
olas como las del agua que llevó
a mis ancestros
a esta isla de sal y caña de azúcar.

gaby comprés

africa

on my right leg,
under my knee,
lives a cinnamon colored stain
that looks a bit like africa
the same way i look a bit like africa
in the shape of my nose
and the waves of my curls
waves like the water that carried
my ancestors in ships
all the way to this island
of salt and sugarcane.

hope

a bird a voice a song
a sun a sunset a heartbeat
a river a sea an ocean
a match a spark a fire
a breath a heart a heartbeat
a raindrop a seed a flower
a word a line a poem
a maker a soul a life

gaby comprés

tu nombre (your name)

tu nombre
i've whispered it into the night
a million times
i've tasted it in mi boca
like honey, slow and sweet
tu nombre
lo sabe la luna
i've sung it to the stars
to my heart
like a lullaby to calm the sea dentro de mí
tu nombre
lo llevo tatuado en los labios
en cada espacio
tu nombre
i've said it like a prayer
lo he llorado
se lo he cantado al alma
hoping it finds peace
tu nombre
is in todas las cosas
está en everything
en el verano
and its rain
in spring y las flores
tu nombre
todo. everything.

if you ever read a poem

the earth will not forget you
for Stacy

i will scream your name
into the sky
until the stars sing it out
and the clouds rain the echoes of my voice
you were here
the earth will not forget you

gaby comprés

there you were
for Rosa Lía

the sky was full of stars tonight.
and among all of them,
there you were.
although you were small,
your light was the brightest
and all the stars stopped to look at you.
the sky was full of stars tonight.
and among all of them,
there you were.
your gentle spirit, your beauty and grace,
shining with the light of all the galaxies.
the sky was full of stars tonight.
and among all of them,
there you were.

if you ever read a poem

thank you

i don't know how long
i'll have you for
how long you'll want to stay
so i'll say
thank you.
thank you for stopping by,
for the lessons you taught me
and the love you gave away,
thank you for the smiles,
the laughter,
the small moments that felt infinite.
thank you for making flowers
in this garden bloom.
thank you for stopping by,
for seeing this soul and thinking
it was worth a visit.

i have learned to measure time

i have learned to measure time
in wednesdays
in laughter
in the smiles we shared together
in midnight text messages
in chocolate chip cookies from Subway
and croquetas
i have learned to measure time
in poetry and coffee cups
in stories and hugs
in plays and words read
but mostly
i have learned to measure time
in the moments we've been together
in the moments i've felt loved
they say time flies
but like this, to me
time is infinite

¿y tu corazón, donde lo dejarás?

¿y tu corazón, donde lo dejarás?
espero que lo dejes en los momentos importantes,
como los amaneceres y atardeceres,
en las risas y las lágrimas,
en los momentos que aprendiste a perdonar,
a soltar y a tomar.
espero que lo dejes en otros corazones también,
que tu luz deje rastros y no se apague,
que no tengas miedo a querer, a caer en brazos de otros,
que no tengas miedo a ser débil y pequeño,
que no tengas miedo a no saberlo todo
para que así te dejes sorprender.

gaby comprés

where will you leave
your heart?

where will you leave your heart?
i hope you leave it in the moments that mattered:
sunrises and sunsets,
laughter and tears,
the moments you learned to forgive,
to hold on and let go.
leave your heart in other hearts,
let your light leave a trail,
do not let it fade,
do not fear love,
do not fear falling in others' arms,
do not fear weakness and smallness
and do not fear not knowing what will happen,
for that is how you let yourself be surprised.

walking waiting wishing

walking
with nothing but hope in my pockets
waiting
to be surprised
and perhaps dazzled
by my life
and the days filled
with what hasn't been yet
wishing
for goodness to follow me
for the spring to bring beauty
for joy.

time

i can't keep time in my hands
i can't make it slow down
i can't make it run faster
i think all that time asks
is for me
to pay attention
to be still
to not change what this moment is
to hold it for as long as it will let me
to try, somehow,
and only sometimes,
to capture it in words and poetry
all that time asks
is for me to be
here

today i mattered

all of this.
this breathing.
this walking.
this speaking.
this writing.
all of this is here
all of this is to say
that i was here.
that i am here,
and when i am no longer here,
i still will be.
all of this
is an attempt
to not forget myself
to not let you forget me.
all of this.
this body.
this hair.
this skin.
this voice.
this space that i am taking.
all of this is here.
all of this, it matters.
today
i mattered.
tomorrow
i will.

gaby comprés

reading poetry in a taxi cab

i am sitting in a taxi cab
reading poetry
and thinking
that there must be some metaphor
hidden here
some deep meaning
something greater than just a woman
reading poetry in a taxi cab
a thought
something like
i am the only one who does this
and that my beauty lives in choosing
poetry to fill my days with
something like
this is what will make someone
fall in love with me
but maybe
maybe the poetry in this moment
maybe the greatest thing in all of this
is that i am a woman
reading poetry in a taxi cab.

love poem for an Uber driver

i wanted to write a poem
about your curls
and how they made my heart
beat like a drum played by a five-year old
who had chocolate cake for lunch
how my fingers were fighting each other
and fighting the urge
to tangle with yours
and make their way to that
chocolate colored head of yours
and get tangled in it too
and i wanted to write a poem
of how much i wanted to be like Cinderella
and leave something behind
with the hopes that you'd call me back
something like a notebook or my
polka-dotted water bottle
but i guess the only thing i left
was a tiny little part of my heart
on the backseat of your car

gaby comprés

hopeless // hopeful

hopeful as i am
i am not a stranger to hopelessness
it is easy to get tired of waiting
for what you want but won't come
like love
like a hand to hold
the time when arms hold you
instead of your arms holding others
like love
like dreams
it is easy to believe what we want will never come
but we keep waiting, don't we?
we wake up every morning,
we give thanks,
we live,
we listen for the song of the birds
and sing back to them, "maybe today,"
and at night when the stars come out
we still dare to make wishes upon them
keeping our options open
hoping
hoping
hoping

alive

i hope
that every evening
after coming home
when i look at myself in the mirror
to find a poem.

to find my curls alive,
to look at them and see the story that today told:
the times the wind kissed the strands
and the hands of those i love touched my head.
the times i laughed and tossed my head back,
unraveling the waves, welcoming the mess,
welcoming the joy.

to find my eyes alive,
tired, maybe, but alive,
that they, too, share the story today told:
the times i closed my eyes in gratitude,
the smiles i smiled with them,
the stars and fire i keep with me,
the shine i cannot erase.

i hope
to look at myself in the mirror,
my face a giveaway
that today i was alive.

gaby comprés

home

and then,
when you don't expect it,
your feet stop wandering.
your soul rests.
your heart breathes.
and
you are home.

if you ever read a poem

daughter // iv

when you leave my body
i will love you
i will tend the spring in your hair
make flowers
bloom
make your waves
oceans
when you leave my body
i will raise you
to the sky
let you touch the clouds
the sun
let you know what light is
when you leave my body
i will keep you in my heart instead
i will kiss your forehead
press you against my chest
i will love you

gaby comprés

beautiful

tell me
i am beautiful
not because i need to hear it
not because if you do not say it i won't believe it
(because i will believe it, i already do)
tell me
i am beautiful
because you think so
because i am

paint me love

paint me yellow
paint me golden
paint me with watercolors
paint me love
paint me poetry
paint me like a starry night
paint me songs
paint me love
paint me sunflowers
paint me light
paint me the sunrise
paint me love

gaby comprés

i love you (te amo)

i love you con todo my heart
te amo with all my voice
te amo como my favorite song
otra vez and again y otra vez
my love for you es como un garden
growing and growing and growing
mi amor is like the sea
deep and hermoso and wild
my love is un poquito como este poema
broken in pedacitos of spanish and inglés
te amo with all mi corazón
i love you con todo my heart

healing in art

there is healing in this,
in you
turning the pain into beauty,
in giving your feelings a voice and words,
in giving your tears color,
turning the rivers that stream down your face
into the paint
that covers your canvas.
there is healing in this,
in making sense of what you are
and what you feel
by making something that wasn't here before
there is healing in this,
in you
making something beautiful of what was not.
there is healing in art.

gaby comprés

i am a poet

i am a poet.
i am not one of your poets.
i did not discover a great truth
(maybe i did)
and i do not write unforgettable words
(maybe i do)
and i use the word 'and' in my poems too much
(i do)
but i am a poet.
my words hold the small truth
of hope.
my words come from no place other than my heart
and together they are a song
that other hearts can sing.
i am a poet
and i am the poem
and i am the words
and i am the heart that beats
behind it all
and my name may be forgotten
but the words i told
will not.
i am a poet,
my kind of poet,
the kind that turns spring into verses
and kindness into a song.

if you ever read a poem

like the stars do

take a picture of this.
of you, of me.
of this moment.
of the way it sits above us
like the stars do with the sky.

gaby comprés

i dream

i dream of new york city.
but not only new york city.
i dream of chicago, of san francisco,
i dream of any city big enough to hold me
and the wildness i carry.
i dream with a love greater than myself,
a love big enough to wrap me in its arms,
a love with grace to forgive my faults.
i dream of the words 'you're beautiful'
sang to me like a song, written in love letters,
tangled in poetry.
i dream of finding myself
of getting lost
and the joy of being found again,
i dream of the words i have yet to write,
the stories i will tell,
the days i don't know.

all the time

i'll want you the way
i want coffee:
in the morning,
in the afternoon,
in the night.
all the time.

gaby comprés

my heart

tonight
the sky was blue and pink
and tinted with gray clouds.
sometimes my heart looks like this too.

if you ever read a poem

a mi esperanza le han salido flores

a mi esperanza
le han salido flores
y no tengo miedo
a lo que no sé.
no puedo esperar a los días que restan
en mi tierra está creciendo la alegría
y las lluvias de primavera no la ahogarán
el sol de verano no la secará
los vientos del otoño no se la llevarán
y el invierno no la matará
a mi esperanza
le han salido flores
y no tengo miedo

gaby comprés

my hope has grown flowers

my hope has grown flowers
and i am not afraid
of what i don't know
and the days, all the days,
they cannot come fast enough
there is wonder growing in this earth
and the seasons will not erase it
the spring rains will not drown it
and the summer sun will not dry it
the autumn winds will not take it
and the winter will not kill it
my hope has grown flowers
and i am not afraid

maleta llena

andaré por el mundo
ligera
con la maleta llena
de recuerdos y café
de los soles y estrellas que vi
los sueños por cumplir
los pasos dados
el aliento robado
andaré por el mundo
y me dejaré perder
por las calles que llevan al amor
y dejaré pedacitos de mí en los lugares
donde mi corazón se enamoró

gaby comprés

i will not pack light

i will travel the world
and i will not pack light,
with a suitcase filled
with memories and coffee,
with the suns and stars i saw,
the steps i gave and the stolen breaths
i will travel the world,
i will get lost
in the streets that lead to love
leaving bits of me in the places
where my heart fell in love

if you ever read a poem

the poetry of life

there is no poetry today,
i said.
but today is the poem.
the laughter, the conversations,
the sharing of beauty,
the seconds that turn into moments
that turn into life
that turn into memories.
isn't time the poetry of life?
isn't the feeling of not having enough words
to tell of the wonder of this day
worth more than a poem?
the seeking and the finding,
the making and the living:
this is the poetry hiding below our feet,
the music we long to sing.

show you love

i will show you love
until the stars fade
and the sun forgets how to shine
i will tell you
you are beautiful and i love you
i love you
i will sing to your soul
write poetry to your heart
i will hold in my hands the love you give me
your vulnerability
i will carry you home

if you ever read a poem

daughter // v

my mother
does not love me in poems
in songs
(the way i know how)
but she loves me in phone calls
and breakfast
and new clothes in december
she loves me in doctor's appointments
and orange juice
and prayer
(the way she knows how)
and i will love you like this too
i will love you like my mother
i will love you like me
i will love you in poetry
in words
in forehead kisses and long hugs
i will braid the words 'you are loved' in your hair
and i will kindle the fires inside you
i will wish upon the stars in your soul
i will love you in dreams
i will love you in ways i cannot tell yet
but i will love you

gaby comprés

i will not love you loudly

i will not love you loudly.
give me a microphone, and i will stutter.
my hands will tremble,
my words will get lost.
i will love you quietly,
in written poems, in soft whispers,
in songs in your ear.
i will tangle my fingers in your hair,
brew you afternoon coffee.
i will read to you in the night,
tell you all my stories.
i will not love you loudly, no,
but i will love you wildly,
beautifully,
quietly,
relentlessly.

if you ever read a poem

the days i want you to keep
for Rafaella

all these days,
the sunshine and the rain,
keep them in your pocket
and take them out to play
when you feel a bit blue
or a little bit gray.

remember how your soul feels
when you do what you love,
when you stop and wonder
at the beauty that's above.

remember how freedom tastes on your lips,
how the heart in your chest flies and skips.
all these days, they will fly,
they are what happens between hello and goodbye.

all these days,
they are what make us,
what makes you you,
what makes me me.
these are the days i want you to keep.

gaby comprés

how else to love

i give you myself
every time i write a poem
every word is a thread from my soul
every letter stands for a heartbeat
i will always have words for you.
i do not know how else to love.

if you ever read a poem

a poem with things i have never told you
for Shiara

the other day,
when you asked if you could take the coffee maker with
you to Boston,
i told you
that i never make coffee
when we are not together.
you laughed.
you jokingly said,
"is it because you miss me when i'm not here?"
we both laughed.
but honestly,
yes.

about a year ago,
you told me,
"you are starting to sound like me!"
i have yet to receive a better compliment.

gaby comprés

the day before i left to new york
you gave me a hat you knitted yourself.
i wore it every day.
(until i lost it on the subway.
i may or may not have cried. i will never say.)

we both know you are not the best speller.
but i love the way you spell love:
s-h-a-r-e,
g-i-v-e,
c-a-r-e.

red shoes
for Andrea

when you gave me your red shoes
i like to think
you also gave me a little bit of yourself.
your bravery,
your spark,
the way you look at life.
i wear them often,
hoping to catch some of your light.
hoping to look a little bit like you.
if i could
i would give everyone a pair of red shoes.
everyone should look like you.

gaby comprés

i will be
for Esther

when the birds in your heart
forget to sing
i will sing to you.
you have sung me back home many times.
for you
i will be
everything you've been to me.
a home,
a river,
a safe place.
when the stars in your soul
begin to dim
i will be your light.
you have been my light many times.
for you
i will be
everything you've been to me.
a lighthouse,
a constellation,
the sun.

i keep you
for Lulu

i keep your laughter in my pockets.
it becomes the sun on rainy days.
i keep your heart inside mine.
yours reminds mine to beat.
i keep you.
i keep you with me.

gaby comprés

a yellow scarf in new york city
for Yomeli

you are
a yellow scarf in new york city
a poem in the subway
a poem in the park
a poem in my heart
you are a poem
and there are not enough words to write you
there is not enough paper
there is not enough ink.

i write you a poem
for Astrid

the day you were born
the sky wrote you a story
using every bit of light
from the sun, moon and stars.
the earth wrote you a song
with wildflowers and lilies
and the laughter of children.
today
i write you a poem,
a gift, a thank you
for all that you are.

gaby comprés

a blessing
for Thalía

may your heart
forever be the house of strength and hope.
may your soul
keep inside a song of bravery.
may you always follow truth
and may love always be your flag.

art and flowers
for María Clara

you are made of art and flowers,
spring and whimsy.
you are a sunshower,
rain and sun
and a rainbow.
you are the song
kindness sings,
the roses beauty grows in her garden.

gaby comprés

traces

there is so much of you here.
in me.
my skin
holds your touch.
your fingerprints are mine.
my eyes
are the color of every coffee we shared.
my lips
have learned to move like yours
my words
rhyme with your own.
do not wonder if you left any traces.
i carry them all.

self-portrait as rain

the april rain.
soft
and full of what hasn't been yet.
of what will be.
the hopeful drops on hopeful seeds.
i am like this.
soft
and full of what hasn't been yet.
hopeful.

gaby comprés

today

the sun came out
and the birds sang
children laughed
and there was music to hear.
there was coffee to brew
and words to share
twinkling eyes
and the summer sent a wave.
you smiled
and i was there.

if you ever read a poem

there is a treasure here

in your brokenness,
i will not leave you.
i will swim to your ocean,
take your wreckage,
and find the beautiful.
we will take the good;
rebuild it.
there is a treasure here.

gaby comprés

so many things

tú eres so many things:
la luz del sun,
las flores de la primavera,
el spring in my step,
las estrellas in my eyes.
la naranja en el morirsoñando,
el olor de mi café,
la esperanza en cada día.
en todas las cosas, there you are.

if you ever read a poem

i hope a poem finds you

i hope a poem finds you
i hope that your moments are
made of words
and your words are
made of moments
i hope a poem finds you
that its beauty never lets you go
that inspiration becomes a companion
a lover, a close friend
i hope a poem finds you,
that its words become your own
that you learn to find inside yourself
what has always been a song.

gaby compris

if you ever read a poem

thank you

There is a line in a poem by Sabrina Benaim that says, 'thank you is the biggest poem I've got inside of me.' It is my hope that my gratitude is always bigger than myself.

Thank you, endlessly, to:

My family, Diego, mami y papi: gracias por apoyarme, a mí y a mis sueños. Gracias por sembrar en mí el amor por las palabras y por dejarlo crecer.

Andrea, Esther, Yomeli, Lulu, Thalía, Astrid & María Clara: Gracias por todo, las risas y los tantos momentos que inspiraron tantos poemas. Gracias por el amor que me han mostrado. No imagino mi vida sin ustedes ni su luz. Las adoro.

Shiara, it means more than I can say to count with your friendship. I look up to you in so many ways and I am so happy your life is a part of mine. Thank you for encouraging my love for words.

Michael, thank you for the poetry, the questions, the books, for introducing me to Mary Oliver, the conversations, and the emails.

Carmen, Manuel & César: the three of you have such a special place in my heart. Thank you for letting my words be a part of your lives.

gaby comprés

Beatriz, esta vez no tuviste que preguntarme si iba a escribir otro libro. Ojalá nunca tengas que preguntarme de nuevo, pero gracias por hacerlo hace casi dos años. Este libro, y todos los que vengan, siempre serán gracias a ti.

Massiel, el del café. Tanto tuyo como mío. Gracias por tanta luz.

Rob, thank you endlessly for always reading my words, no matter how small they are. Your kindness makes choosing vulnerability a bit easier.

Estefanía, gracias por el amor con que recibes mis palabras, por la luz que me has dado, por creer en este libro y en las palabras que lo llenan.

Rafaella, even from far away, you inspired so much of what's in these pages. I love you.

Taylor, thank you for making this book beautiful.

Charissa, thank you for being my biggest cheerleader. For loving every poem, every word. For always believing.

Nilsa, gracias for everything. for your words, your encouragement and light.

the beautiful friends I've made on the internet: thank you, a thousand times, for the kind words, the encouragement and the love you give me daily. It is a joy to share my words with you. They are for you.

if you ever read a poem

to everyone who reads my poems: it is the joy of my life to share my words with you and that you choose to take them. Thank you for opening your hearts to me and for letting me open my heart to you. I hope these words make you smile. I hope they make you feel less alone.

gaby comprés

notes

The poem *maybe love is in new york city*, on page 41, was inspired by the lines "maybe love is in New York City already asleep. You are in California, Australia, wide awake." from the poem 'when love arrives' by Sarah Kay and Phil Kaye.

every flower, on page 44, is inspired by a line from Sabrina Benaim's poem 'first date'. The line reads: "My body is a garden rooted in gratitude. 'Thank you' is the biggest poem I've got inside of me.'

The poem *mosaic heart,* on page 71, was a request from my friend Yomeli.

you've always been there, on page 74, is inspired by my 11th grade English teacher, Wayne Hammond. During a conversation when I went to show him my book, I told him that I had changed a lot over the years, to which he replied, "oh no, you've always been there".

The poem *this is all free,* on page 78, is my first attempt at found poetry. The words come from the book *A Child of Books* by Oliver Jeffers and Sam Winston. It is my favorite picture book.

if you ever read a poem

quiero darte una canción, on page 80, was written for my friend Denisse Cruz. It was inspired by one of her writing pieces.

The poem *keep my heart,* on page 91, was written for my friends before they left for Spain in the fall of 2017. In my second book, there are color poems for each of my friends. In this poem, I included the colors of their individual poems: green, yellow and gold.

the milk to my coffee, on page 128, was written as a response to a Rupi Kaur poem, 'the sun and her sunflowers'.

I wrote the poem *hope,* on page 138, after reading a poem my friend Michael wrote, in an attempt at imitating his fantastic piece.

tu nombre (your name), on page 139, was my first attempt at a poem that was in both English and Spanish. It started as a silly poem and it turned out to be a very beautiful one.

The poem *the earth will not forget you,* on page 140, was written in memory of Stacy Fulford, an actress and beautiful human I never got to meet, but whose passing impacted me.

gaby comprés

i have learned to measure time, on page 143, was written to my friends Andrea and Esther.

The poem *time,* on page 147, was inspired by a poem my friend Esther wrote about time: *¿Qué es el tiempo?*

love poem for an Uber driver, on page 150, was written to a particularly handsome Uber driver. It was the first love poem I wrote, and it was a poem I was unsure belonged in this collection, but it is a favorite of my readers, as well as mine.

The poem *alive,* on page 152, was a request from my friend Andrea. I loved writing it.

home, on page 153, was written on my twenty-first birthday. I spent my birthday night surrounded by people I spent a very long time praying and hoping for. Being with them on such a special day felt like coming home.

The poem *the days i want you to keep,* on page 172, borrows its title from a book one of my first students, Rafaella, wrote. Her book's title was inspired by my second book's title, *the words i want you to keep.*

about the author

Gaby Comprés is an educator and poet from Santo Domingo who was born in 1996. Inspired by nature, people and her own experiences, she has been writing poetry since March 2014. Her work has been published in several magazines, including Grafted Magazine and Majesty. She published her first poetry collection, *A Song of Bravery,* in March 2015, at the age of eighteen. Her second collection, *the words i want you to keep,* was published in June 2017. When she is not writing, she is reading and thinking about writing.

You can find Gaby on Instagram and Twitter at @gabywrites, where she tries not to overshare her poetry.

Made in the USA
Las Vegas, NV
16 March 2022

45800300R00115